*

many waters   cannot
quench hope –

- Jen Hadfield

FOUNDED BY T.S. ELIOT 1953

SPRING 2021 NO. 268

CONTENTS

CHOICE

RECOMMENDATIONS

SPECIAL COMMENDATION

TRANSLATION CHOICE

PAMPHLET CHOICE

WILD CARD

Poetry Book Society

CHOICE SELECTORS RECOMMENDATION SPECIAL COMMENDATION	SINÉAD MORRISSEY & ANDREW McMILLAN
TRANSLATION SELECTOR	ILYA KAMINSKY
PAMPHLET SELECTORS	MARY JEAN CHAN & NICK MAKOHA
WILD CARD SELECTOR	ANTHONY ANAXAGOROU
CONTRIBUTORS	SOPHIE O'NEILL NATHANIEL SPAIN KYM DEYN
EDITORIAL & DESIGN	ALICE KATE MULLEN

Poetry Book Society Memberships

Choice

4 Books a Year: 4 Choice books & 4 *Bulletins* (UK £55, Europe £65, ROW £75)

World

8 Books: 4 Choices, 4 Translation books & 4 *Bulletins* (£98, £120, £132)

Charter

20 Books: 4 Choices, 16 Recommendations & 4 *Bulletins* (£180, £210, £235)

Complete

24 Books: 4 Choices, 16 Recommendations, 4 Translations & 4 *Bulletins* (£223, £265, £292)

Single copies of the *Bulletin* £9.99

Cover Art 'Taigh' by Alec Finlay, published 2014.
Photograph by Hannah Devereux www.hannahdevereux.com
Copyright Poetry Book Society and contributors. All rights reserved.
ISBN 9781913129255 ISSN 0551-1690

Poetry Book Society | Milburn House | Dean Street | Newcastle upon Tyne | NE1 1LF
0191 230 8100 | enquiries@poetrybooksociety.co.uk

WWW.POETRYBOOKS.CO.UK

LETTER FROM THE PBS

2021 has got off to an inauspicious start, however at the time of writing the world has been inspired by the words of Amanda Gorman, performing her poetry at the US Presidential Inauguration, reminding me once again how powerful and democratic poetry really is; a girl of twenty two, stealing the show and wowing the world with her own poetry at the most tense of presidential inaugurations. I find this a huge symbol of hope.

A warm welcome to the Spring PBS *Bulletin*, spreading hope in our own small way and bringing a poetic slice of joy to our members! Congratulations to Jen Hadfield as this season's Choice with *The Stone Age*, exploring human relationships with the world around us and each other. The Spring selections criss-cross the world and the range of human experience; profound, moving and thought-provoking. I hope you are as inspired to read the selected and reviewed collections as we are.

There are some sad farewells and welcomes to make note of. This is Sinéad Morrisey's final set of selections before handing the baton to the wonderful Sarah Howe. A huge thank you to Sinéad not only for her insightful commentary, but also her personal support of all our PBS endeavours! This is also Ilya Kaminsky's final set of selections and again, Ilya has been hugely influential on how we select our translated books. So thank you Ilya for helping to increase the range of translated titles on offer. We look forward to welcoming Loretta Collins Klobah in the summer.

We will continue with our series of virtual online events with an exciting array of partners and poets, including Kendal Poetry Festival and NCLA. Please check our social media or events page for updates on who, when and where. And we're delighted that Andrew McMillan is continuing our online bookclub into 2021. It has been a source of real delight for so many since its launch in May.

You know where we are if you need us – we look forward to hearing from you and sharing our love of poetry in 2021!

SOPHIE O'NEILL
PBS & INPRESS DIRECTOR

JEN HADFIELD

Jen Hadfield's fourth poetry collection *The Stone Age* explores neurodiversity. Passionately involved with the wild world, she uses poetry, lyrical essay and, occasionally, sculpture in cast porcelain, to try and share her intense experience of the here-and-now. She is also working on *Storm Pegs*, a collection of essays about Shetland, where she lives. Her work has garnered numerous awards, including the 2008 T.S. Eliot Prize for *Nigh-No-Place* (Bloodaxe). Jen has performed her work internationally, attending festivals and residencies in Iraq, New Zealand and Canada. She is a Creative Writing Teaching Fellow at Glasgow University and is building a house in Shetland, very slowly.

THE STONE AGE

PICADOR | £10.99 | PBS PRICE £8.25

In the final poem of *The Stone Age,* the speaker discovers her shadow "in the / corner of your kitchen", "fat / and glossy, full as a tick." Gaps – between the self and its shadow, between things and our names for them, between humans and rocks – are this collection's central concern, while the act of pitching poetry into such fissures produces a dazzling display of possible approximations.

> Fear opens
> a cave in your brain –

> I c o l o u r it in with
> intimate cr yst als.

"I know you can tell I'm translating / as I go," confesses the speaker in 'Gaelic', and the contingency of utterance is manifested elsewhere in typographical play. Truncated attempts to speak truthfully ("to be honest with you—", "to be quite frank—", "I have to admit—") are swallowed by the triumph of white space / silence, while the diction of standing stones, which Hadfield inhabits as convincingly as Les Murray inhabits the diction of pigs, is signalled by irregular letter size, font, spacing and line-breaks (impossible to replicate here). A weirded lyric brilliance is the result, "a song of unsettling / grace" ('Hardanger Fiddle and Nyckelharpa') which is profoundly connected to the language, music, history, geology and flora of Shetland.

Differences between stone time and human time inevitably generate different languages as decorous poems with titles are consistently interrupted by the non-human addressing us back:

> Because my sentence
> is lava-s l ow
> andsometimesmangl ed...

Throughout, Hadfield contrasts our species' firework brevity with the "deep / time" of the Earth. But the sense of slowed-down time, of taking one's time, of the author simply standing still and looking, is also everywhere in evidence. "Thirty years ago, as this poem began" begins 'Umbrella'. *The Stone Age* has been well worth the wait.

 SINÉAD MORRISSEY

JEN HADFIELD

"It looks like something's wrong with you", the speaker says to a mountain hare, in my poem 'Snowline'. This was the first time I was aware of writing about neurodiversity. I've worried about that line ever since. What if you thought I really meant it?

As a woman with quite a few of the traits associated with Asperger's Syndrome, I worry about truth and misunderstanding a lot. But, uncomfortably, I left the line in: it sums up the way many people still think of diversity. We have this difficult habit of plotting human consciousness on a continuum between the poles of "most and least normal". Even "neurodiverse" has "neurotypical" as its binary opposite. But what if we call humankind "neurodiverse" by definition?

The Stone Age is my way of understanding my place here on earth, a niche somewhere between the human and wild. Shetland is so often the cusp between those places. It's also a linguistic niche. I've been imagining the consciousness of cliffs, sea-slugs, of constructed things like gates and strimmers. My neurodiverse mind makes that easier for me to do.

Then I wanted to write intimately about an even more unlikely phenomenon: people understanding each other. There are quite a few poems here about struggling to speak. I think that's ok. A poem is made of two things: words, and silent words. This book is riddled with the latter: as hesitation, interruption, suggestion, the palpable unsaid.

It also feels timely to articulate inarticulacy. Increasingly, I hear the growl – like distant sea-surge – of what our "leaders" are leaving unsaid... about Coronavirus, Brexit, climate crisis, habitat loss and extinction.

And we the quiet-and-stumbling-spoken also go unheard... like the stones in this collection, who love brief and hasty humankind, and are telling us so, if we could only listen.

JEN RECOMMENDS

Em Strang, whose sequence 'The Bog-Eye of the Human', in *Antlers of Water* is a beguiling guide to other ways of being in the wild world. I'm desperate for James Goodman's edgy and beautiful *Stone Fairy Mountain Shrimp* – with its praise poems and experimental elegies for lost and endangered species – to find the publisher it deserves. Some of the poems can be found in *Magma* and *The Rialto*. And John Glenday – the master of the unspoken – his new *Selected Poems* came out with Picador in 2020.

GYÖ

You tell me people like me don't have feelings. And you
wonder why I don't call myself a person. I say rage is a cold
cliff, longing, a skerry. Pleasure is a kelp-hung arch, glittered
constantly by the licking of the wave. Tenderness is a
sandbar. Joy an overhang of shiversome schist. You navigate
the arch, the skerry, – you land, cast off: you take a pleasure
cruise; a stripped feather twirls on the oily swell, the sea-
stack recedes into heavy, bright mist. But I'm the quartz, the
basalt, the gabbro. And if I had children like people have
children, I would creche them in a daisied gentleness, they'd
fledge from the gargling daycare of the gyö –

LIMPET

Stop, now you're
home, and consider
what that feels like —
don't stop, continue

to whirl, an introvert
tornado, across the
flooded rockpool
in an ease of gypsy

skirts — cyclonic,
high and wet. This
is not a thing
to sit tight upon —

locked to your home-
scar against the
migraine of the waves —
this rebate will wait

that you can spin home to
like cup to saucer —
matching every chip
in your shell to its

own rocky rostrum.
Clamp down —
turn the key of
yourself in the lock

of yourself, fasten —
with a hundred
infinitesimal
mortices —

Image: Martin Figura

TIFFANY ATKINSON

Tiffany Atkinson is the author of four poetry collections including *Kink and Particle* (Seren, 2006), a PBS Recommendation and winner of the Jerwood Aldeburgh First Collection Prize; *Catulla et al* (Bloodaxe, 2011), a *TLS* Book of the Year and shortlisted for the Wales Book of the Year; and *So Many Moving Parts* (Bloodaxe, 2014), a PBS Recommendation and winner of the Roland Mathias Poetry Prize. She is currently working on a book about poetry, ethics and embarrassment. Tiffany is a Leverhulme Research Fellow and Professor of Creative Writing (Poetry) at the University of East Anglia.

LUMEN

BLOODAXE | £10.99 | PBS PRICE £8.25

In the quest to do justice to the lived-experience of chronic pain and to find a language for that which is so often beyond the limits of language, Atkinson, in the opening sequence 'Dolorimeter', turns towards both medical phraseology and the poetic image in order to bring about a fresh perspective. The sequence begins:

> Dolorimetry has been defined
> as 'the measurement of pain sensitivity
> or pain intensity'. See *inter alia*: reliability.
> We might also call it language.

Elsewhere we are shown the way pain can inhabit the day-to-day lives of those who live with it:

> In the house the pain hung like laundry from each edge.
> You could walk in and feel it flap against your face

Through found, collaged poetry or, at one point, a questionnaire, the poems weigh what language might be necessary to find that "lumen" of the title which, in one definition, is an opening in the body.

As the book moves on into its other sections, that understanding of the self and the body is placed into different situations, a yoga session or a creative writing class. In the poem 'It is a very gracious hotel', we get the wonderfully moving final moment:

> I've been the chandeliers and windows full of sheep
> and green resources   It is my life   a very gracious hotel

It brings the whole poem tumbling inside the self, what began as a misunderstanding and unravels and grows from there.

The final poem of the collection, 'Eggshell', gives us Atkinson's flare for the image: ("Up the slowly gleaming conch of staircase") and slowly dismantles the syntax of an artistic domestic scene to great effect. We get the phrase "Each body's quiet / business", and be that love, embarrassment, art or pain, these poems are able to find new language to articulate that work.

12   ANDREW McMILLAN

TIFFANY ATKINSON

The opening sequence in *Lumen* began as the documenting of a short writer's residency in my local hospital. But as I began writing, a more open and exploratory work emerged as my own experiences, and those of the people I talked to, began to muddle my "documentary" intentions. The clash of the literal and lateral is something explored explicitly in several poems, like 'McGill Pain Questionnaire (Annotated)' for example. The actual questionnaire – a published table of adjectives for classifying pain – has been criticised for unhelpful hairsplitting (how do we distinguish between "pulsing" and "throbbing", for example)?

This point might prove Elaine Scarry's famous axiom (1985) that pain is fundamentally resistant to language. Yet the linguistic flair with which people described their experiences made me think rather the contrary: that you might choose any number of apparently unrelated adjectives and apply them creatively, and accurately, to pain. This poem, mimicking the form of the Questionnaire, includes a mix of "official" and rogue adjectives, allowing the reader to decide which apply, and perhaps suggesting that language – what else do we have, after all – is more supple, and certainly more playful, than theory would have us believe. This hope underpins all of these poems.

In the end, the poems in *Lumen* are not a sequence or collection so much as a sample of "readings", from both within the hospital and without. They take the dolorimeter (a hypothetical pain-measuring device) as a motif for an essentially incomplete and provisional effort: one that draws on multiple voices, forms and registers to plead language's "unreliability" as the very source of new patterns of thought and understanding. Since we have bodies and language in common, this is something exciting to work with.

TIFFANY RECOMMENDS

Carolyn Forché, *In the Lateness of the World* (Bloodaxe); Peter Gizzi, *Sky Burial: New and Selected Poems* (Carcanet); Richard Gwyn, *The Other Tiger: Recent Poetry from Latin America* (Seren); David Jones, *In Parenthesis* (Faber); Bhanu Kapil, *How To Wash A Heart* (Pavilion Poetry); Kei Miller, *In Nearby Bushes* (Carcanet); Marianne Moore, *Observations* (FSG) and Gertrude Stein, *Tender Buttons* (City Lights Books).

feel the heart-stone hit
the bottom of that lake

A LINE FROM THE DOCTOR (ANNOTATED)

We are trying to avoid the word *pain*
It is far too full of itself   This

is less a problem of language
than a problem of belief

Anyone can tolerate a small scratch
Anyone can manage their discomfort

but tug on the root of *peine* /

                        poena /
                            poine

who knows what you might drag up

and blood-feud   judgment   hellfire   torment
these are no longer medical concerns

Keep the language clean and well-lit
Leave its shadows swinging on the gate

YOUSIF M. QASMIYEH

Yousif M. Qasmiyeh was born and educated in Baddawi refugee camp in North Lebanon. He is currently completing a DPhil on containment and the archive in "refugee writing" at the University of Oxford's English Faculty. Time, the body, and ruination inform his poetry and prose. His poetry and translations have appeared in journals and magazines including *Modern Poetry in Translation, Stand, Critical Quarterly, GeoHumanities* and *Cambridge Literary Review*. Yousif is Creative Encounters Editor of the *Migration and Society* journal, Writer-in-Residence of the Refugee Hosts research project, and Joint Lead of the Imagining Futures Baddawi Camp Lab.

WRITING THE CAMP

BROKEN SLEEP BOOKS | £10.99 | PBS PRICE £8.25

One of the dazzling things that this collection is able to do so well is use the poetic line and the stanza to mould time into something spherical rather than linear, something lived in rather than moved through. 'The dinghy', for example, opens: "When the dinghy started to sink, nobody knew what to do." This is followed a few lines later by:

I knew one of them.

We met in Manchester.

When we last spoke on the phone, after his asylum claim was rejected, he sounded very down.

The horrific incident of the sinking dinghy, the meeting in Manchester, the phone call, the rejected asylum claim, all exist somehow together, in the lived experience of a life which carries its history with it as it tries to build a new future.

There is a directness to the voice of these poems, combined with an ability to frankly consider the status of the refugee or asylum-seeker, as in 'Non-Arrival':

The moment I arrive, I want to come back.

I never knew why reaching a place has always meant the
end of my place.

Whether I walk, travel by bus or train, or fly, I would only be
there to mark the occasion of coming back.

Non-arrival, I suppose, can also be another occasion.

The use of collective or singular pronouns, rather than specific names, emphasises how little we know of the lives of people too-often dismissed by hateful newspaper headlines. That directness of voice gives us astonishing moments of revelation that lodge themselves in the reader's mind:

Translating one's name into another environment can make
the actual name less valid.

This is a searing and vital collection that deserves as wide a readership as possible.

 ANDREW McMILLAN

YOUSIF M. QASMIYEH

In Arabic, my mother tongue, the word *lugha* (language) is inherently deficient. According to the 10th century scholar Al-Azhari, its very existence is predicated on a deficient noun. The collision between completeness and incompleteness in the Arabic language is, in turn, implicitly echoed in Gilles Deleuze and Félix Guattari's articulation of writing as both a translation and a dismantling of the same assemblages. It is to this premise that my writing continually returns.

Indeed, what might be seen as language is also its ever-enduring incompleteness wedged between the written and the oral as two furrows in the same field. In Baddawi refugee camp, my place of birth, writing becomes a process of injecting time with time: hunting down my illiterate mother's words, either by retracing them in scattered fragments or by dismembering their original sites, as she recounts the multiply-recounted tales of tomorrow, and my father's unpublished texts whose rhymes and imageries are those of an eternal child deprived of age and time.

In *Writing the Camp*, I also write for myself, in a stranger's language, the poetry which is suspicious of itself and its surroundings: the stranger's mispronounced vowels. To quote Jacques Derrida, in this context I write my conversion into an origin; "to translate [myself] (*convertere*) into [English]": writing the tremor, as both a happening and a consequence, an uncoincidental pulse taking me back to the inexhaustive in memory and the body.

Paying particular attention to the incomplete, being, time, dwelling, camps, dialects, refugees, the body and the archive, *Writing the Camp* sits precisely on the threshold, clustering fragments with the unintentional integrity of a sequence. If I were to grant these fragments a name, I would say: they are poems, in the unorthodox sense, conceived in various times but also about different times in a refugee's life, and about their afterlives and the discarded in living.

YOUSIF RECOMMENDS

Natalie Diaz, *Postcolonial Love Poem* (Faber); Ricky Ray, *Quiet, Grit, Glory* (Broken Sleep Books) and *The Sound of the Earth Singing to Herself* (Fly on the Wall Press); Vahni Capildeo, *Odyssey Calling* (Sad Press); Mina Gorji, *Art of Escape* (Carcanet); David Constantine, *Belongings* (Bloodaxe); Jamie McKendrick, *The Years* (Arc); Theophilus Kwek, *Moving House* (Carcanet); Jane Lovell, *This Tilting Earth* (Seren Books); Michael Hofmann, *One Lark, One Horse* (Faber) and Jennifer Edgecombe, *The Grief of The Sea* (Broken Sleep Books).

FINGERPRINTING

She did to me what a friend would normally do for a friend
or a lover for another lover - she held my hand very tightly.

When I looked at her, my fingers were above the scanner -
my flesh was scanned and so was the air around us.

I thought of looking her in the eye again, pretending that
we were in love and in that room where asylum-seekers
and suspects gather it was our opportunity to embrace one
another while the machine was doing its job.

I gave my fingerprints and left.

Every time I think of that moment I feel the need to go back
to that terminal and ask her what it meant to touch a
stranger.

PAST TENSE

They asked him to strip off all of his clothes while discussing his asylum claim.

The uniform was loose on him – two sizes bigger to accommodate his solitude.

The being is being strangled somewhere nearby.

On their way to court they disposed of him and his documents.

He never paid any attention to numbers.

They called it his room so he could commit suicide in private.

The last time they called his name he was not there.

His shoes had new soles.

He enjoyed photographing feet, including his own.

His title was written in bold.

His name looked faint.

The interviewer failed to conjugate a verb in the past tense.

He opted for the present tense instead.

He saw *term*, *term*inate and *term*inal on the same page.

He landed unscathed.

His only injury was mental.

In the end, he claimed asylum.

Image: Sue Kwon

ROWAN RICARDO PHILLIPS

Rowan Ricardo Phillips is the author of two books of poems, *Heaven* and *The Ground*, and two essay collections, *The Circuit* and *When Blackness Rhymes with Blackness*. As well as being a finalist for the Griffin Poetry Prize, his awards include a Whiting Award, the PEN/Joyce Osterweil Award for Poetry, the Anisfield-Wolf Book Award, the PEN/ESPN Award for Literary Sports Writing and the Nicolás Guillén Outstanding Book Award. Phillips lives in New York City and Barcelona.

LIVING WEAPON

FABER | £10.99 | PBS PRICE £8.25

We begin in the sky above New York. The speaker has wings, a human-angel, at pains to communicate the specifics of this secret, suspended place: "The first blue aspects of the sky at his hour are unreasonably beautiful, like the colour of that colour in a cube of ice."

Throughout *Living Weapon* Phillips connects the transcendent with the precise, lived details of human existence in poems of stunning philosophical sophistication and descriptive grace.

Imagery of the cosmos is threaded all the way through – planets, suns, the Big Bang – and if "sun after sun after sun comes / Back to us slightly more cracked at the core; / Because experience is translation", racism and police violence are powerfully addressed as factors of elemental degradation. 'Mortality Ode' describes a trip to a mobile phone shop and the miasma of danger that emanates from police officers who call in as casual customers:

> ...his right hand hip-high
> And resting on the pimpled, black, blunt
> End of his piece as he walks, like all of them,
> Unbalanced but propped up by strange gravity...

In 'Obsolete Machinery' interplanetary exploration is contrasted with a fascist march through Charlottesville:

> Wake up! We've sent tin cans
> Past Neptune. It's the twenty-first century.

All of which has profound implications for poetic expression. Phillips neatly upends T.S. Eliot's privileged critical musings: "I wandered through each chartered street / Till I was shot by the police" ('Tradition and the Individual Talent'), and instead posits a radical aesthetic transforming "that poem your father / Wrote you" into a "living weapon." "A ruined expression / of pure poetry. A pure expression / Of ruined poetry. Either will do," declares the speaker in 'The Lunatic, The Lover, and The Poet', meaning poetry is still possible, but on urgent, revitalised terms.

 SINÉAD MORRISSEY

SELECTOR'S COMMENT

ROWAN RICARDO PHILLIPS

Seamus Heaney's *Field Work* was an inspiration for this book.

I am always in conversation with the poetic canon in one way or another and *Living Weapon's* point of entry to that conversation is particularly pointed, the notes sharper, the social self an innate element of the voice as it searches for beauty and meaning in a world that too often and too quickly offers what is ugly and what is meaningless to the mind in search of something greater than itself.

An angle of entry into this book was my love of both great civic poetry and love poems. *Living Weapon* deliberately seeks to forge something out of this love: something with which to step further into the world. Hopefully that something forged is well-wrought, balanced and bright enough to lead a reader towards the light.

In *Living Weapon*, I veer from the spiritual and monastic tones of my prior book of poems, *Heaven* (FSG, 2015) – just as *Heaven* had veered from the longing, eidetic lyrics of my first book of poems, *The Ground* (FSG, 2012) – in order to create, in this latest book, a poetry collection of social force written in the key signature of the poetic canon, which like life itself is capacious, open-ended, and problematic. Prose poems bookend *Living Weapon*. They are meditations that look forward and back, like Paul Klee's *Angelus Novus*, about which Walter Benjamin wrote: "This is how one pictures the angel of history. His face is turned toward the past. Where we perceive a chain of events, he sees one single catastrophe which keeps piling wreckage upon wreckage and hurls it in front of his feet. The angel would like to stay, awaken the dead, and make whole what has been smashed."

Amen to that.

ROWAN RECOMMENDS

Karen McCarthy Woolf, *Seasonal Disturbances* (Carcanet); Valzhyna Mort, *Music for the Dead and Resurrected* (FSG); Alice Oswald, *Nobody* (Cape); Ishion Hutchinson, *House of Lords and Commons* (Faber); Sharon Olds, *Odes* (Cape); Natalie Diaz, *Postcolonial Love Poem* (Faber); M. NourbeSe Philip, *Zong* (Silver Press); Nick Laird, *Feel Free* (Faber); Ovid, *Metamorphoses*; Zoë Hitzig, *Mezzanine* (Ecco); Aaron Fagan, *A Better Place Is Hard to Find* (The Song Cave); J.V. Foix, *Sol, i de dol* (Quaderns Crema); Melcion Mateu, *Illes lligades* (LaBreu).

HALO

We wander round ring after ring of life,
One after another, blossoms of light
To which we're but a mere flotsam of bees.

And although this isn't true, the poem says
This is true; life, light, flowers and bee: truths.
So stop and hold this poem above your head.

Hold it up to whatever light you find.
Then let it go: forget it, if you can.
If it is meant to remain it will remain.

And if it is meant to light, it will light.
Your hands will have moved on to something else
But your head will have, say it, its halo.

NIGHT OF THE ELECTION

Then, Seamus Heaney's poem – suddenly – gone,
The words became a thing looked at, not read.
But then those, too, went the way of Patrón,
Blanketing whatever dim light November
Had let in. In the poem's place an oyster
Appeared on a plate: languid, the color
Of vanilla, moist fennel, raw silver,
Crushed hay, sunk ships, quince and Jupiter,
Flexing taut, then slack, then taut in its shell;
How, with all that had happened, it managed
To be there, the gorged bulb glistening, well,
Here's where I'd tell you... but a ghoulish
Creamsicle flavor ruined the moment,
A sad irrelevance now relevant.

ROWAN RICARDO PHILLIPS

Image: Urszula Soltys

MICHAEL SYMMONS ROBERTS

Michael Symmons Roberts was born in Preston, Lancashire in 1963. He has published six collections of poetry and received a number of accolades including the Forward Prize, the Costa Poetry Award and the Whitbread Poetry Prize. As a librettist, his work has been performed in concert halls and opera houses around the world. An award-winning broadcaster and dramatist, he has published two novels, and is Professor of Poetry at Manchester Metropolitan University. He is also a Fellow of the Royal Society of Literature.

RANSOM

CAPE | £10.00 | PBS PRICE £7.50

Ransom weaves a web of tangled obsessions, including imprisonment, mortality, conflict and the visual arts, across four discreet sections. We open in the dystopian present of 24-hour surveillance and digital espionage. In 'Ware' (itself a pun on warfare/wares) a disembodied voice addresses the defrauded:

> Think of your data
> not as seized, but read and understood
> so deeply that your goods
>
> and ours, are one

While in 'The Tears of Things' (itself a play on ripping and crying):

> My neighbour leaves home and walks out of shot,
>
> his progress handed from camera
> to camera until the land runs out.

Surreal stories abound, delivered in dead-pan first-person narrative, while the anguish of 'Episodics', which chronicles the death of a beloved parent in angular syntax, is the backbone of the book. 'Vingt Regards' fuses occupied Paris, the codes of the Resistance and impending Liberation with the French composer Olivier Messiaen's *Vingt Regards sur L'Enfant Jésus* – though again a strength of the sequence is Roberts' talent for uncanny atmospherics: the conjuring of pervasive but intangible threat. Even in aftermath, things are not as one imagined. The released prisoner, who never understands what happened, finds himself "some quaking stranger holed up / in a rented room above a betting shop."

Against this unremitting backdrop, a hunger for the transcendent is carefully acknowledged and articulated. The final poem in the numinous sequence 'Takk', inspired by the paintings of Jake Attree and published as a chapbook by Fine Press Poetry, describes "plane trees, scabbed and patched as dogs" all the better to "flourish here [...] to rise again, / naked but unflinched."

"I am aware of a song, / but can't make out the words as yet" is the collection's closing statement. In the terrifying world of *Ransom*, this seems more than enough.

SINÉAD MORRISSEY

MICHAEL SYMMONS ROBERTS

The title *Ransom* came when around half the poems were finished or taking shape. The word seemed to make sense – to me at least – of the territory these new poems were exploring, albeit from very different angles. *Ransom* as in ransomware, ransom theory, incarnation and atonement, captivity and release, liberty and limit.

It brought me back to a focus on the body as (in the philosopher Ludwig Wittgenstein's phrase) "the best picture of the human soul." Wittgenstein's thinking about the corporeal and Simone Weil's ideas on necessity and love were with me in the making of these poems, as were wider cultural takes on "ransom", from gangster movies, games, songs. The poems began to pull in shadow boxes, security cameras and horses' heads.

Then came Olivier Messiaen's *Vingt Regards*. His visionary set of piano pieces about the nativity – a story of captivity and release if ever there was one – were composed in occupied Paris in 1944 and completed just after the city was liberated. That music led me into making a series of poems on incarnation, each poem a scene in an imagined film being shot in the rooms and streets of wartime Paris under curfew.

My final months of work on this collection coincided with the first UK Covid lockdown in Spring through Summer 2020, giving the notions of ransom, captivity and release an immediacy which found its way into some of the poems. The final sequence – 'Takk' – is an attempt at a kind of poem I've always found to be the hardest to write with authenticity – a poem of praise.

MICHAEL RECOMMENDS ——————————————

My reading in the last year has included fine new collections by Rachel Mann, Will Harris, Martha Sprackland and Seán Hewitt, plus returns to the selecteds and collecteds of Gwendolyn Brooks, Marianne Moore and Anna Akhmatova. A commission to adapt two great elegies for BBC Radio meant weeks spent getting lost in the lines of Milton's *Lycidas* and Tennyson's *In Memoriam* and in both cases I feel I've barely scratched the surface.

If the things of the world are crying
it cannot be to honour us,

I SAW ETERNITY THE OTHER NIGHT

As dusk outside began to steep,
I sat and waited for the shapes

of rooftops, geese, mill chimneys,
to soften as my window

pulled the world outside to in.
Self-portrait in a dim-lit room,

the street outside turned mirror
and my eyes reflected back as clear,

as simple, guileless as a dog's gaze.
Distemperate, I will not rise

tonight to my TV's illumined bait,
since all its shows, to captivate,

are cut and scripted with a sleight
to draw me in, then to spring shut.

Sleep now, replace this maudlin scene,
with one vast flawless empty screen

of screen in screen in screen in screen.

NEW POETRIES VIII ANTHOLOGY

CARCANET | £14.99 | PBS PRICE £11.25

The plural in the title is important for this quarter's Special Commendation, it speaks to the range of different voices on offer, and, with a spectrum of ages and publishing history in other genres, also challenges that stereotype so often put forward in writing that "new" must mean "young".

There isn't space to do justice to all the twenty three poets in such a short blurb, each one of which is given a short bio after their selection for eager readers to seek out more of their work, alongside space at the beginning of their selection to sketch out a mini manifesto or *ars poetica* on their influences and hoped-for directions in their work.

That plurality of voice makes it hard to make sweeping generalisations; there is the continued return of the long poem, perhaps as antidote to the perceived shortening of our attention spans, and yet just as many short and concise glimpses. There are poems seeking to use the entirety of the page, through breath space, and tabulation, through exploring the potential of the long line, and yet there are poets who make a great virtue of the staccato, short, sharp, few words as well.

In the past, when I've had the rare treat of appearing in an anthology, I've always been disappointed when the reviewer singles out a few key people and failed to mention me (Oh the ego of the poet!) and so I'm loath to do that here.

Suffice to say that this is a selection of poets which has benefitted from the different eyes of the anthology editors Michael Schmidt and John McAuliffe (the latter of which I, perhaps erroneously, credit with the inclusion of the exciting Irish names who are present) and all of whom, if we didn't know before, we will know when they make their own indelible mark on poetry in the years to come.

  ANDREW McMILLAN

QUARANTINE (AN EXTRACT) BY PARWANA FAYYAZ

In the slowest pace of the unknown times
My father's hand caresses his headless cellphone.
He wakes me to tell me.
Times are uncertain. The legless virus is deadly.

His words in the invisible wire reach me
In between love and worry.
In summary, he says.
Take care of yourself.

Through the sunless sky his flawless voice echoes
Clear memories from wartime.
Stuck in the basement,
A father and his daughter are laying, foreheads on the ground.

My arms fall restful on the chair,
Or perhaps they are losing their
Pleasure of pain to numbness –
Like raw salmon served cold.

The only visitor from home comes in its best attire,
The moon in ivory color.
I appeal. I pray.
At least the pregnant Venus should change its color. Perhaps to red.

The night does not listen to me,
Nor to the owl that has taken up a room
On my bed.
It too is worried in its stuffed skin.

WAR OF THE BEASTS AND THE ANIMALS
MARIA STEPANOVA, TRANS. SASHA DUGDALE

BLOODAXE | £12.00 | PBS PRICE £9.00

Wildly experimental, and yet movingly traditional. Ironic, and yet obsessed with spell-making. Full of allusions to various different canonical voices, and yet heart-wrenchingly direct. What, friends, is this? It's that glorious thing: the poetry of Maria Stepanova. So many poems here are in response to crisis (war in Ukraine or World War I), but they aren't exactly typical war elegies:

> on the twenty-second of june
> at four o'clock on the dot
> I won't be listening to anything
> I'll have my eyes shut
>
> I'll bury the foreign broadcast
> It's the news but I won't lift a hand
> If anyone comes I'm out of the loop
>
> I'm a sparrow   I'm no man's land.

The 22nd of June 1941 is the day Germany invaded the USSR. One overhears many such echoes to crisis. But it's the "overhearing" that counts here, not just the story; it is the scattered orchestra that keeps playing during the fire that these pages most resemble:

> the home fires are burning low
> be still my heart beat slow.

The translator Sasha Dugdale does a truly stunning job in bringing these wild, soaring, unexpected orchestral fragments into English:

> I saw the skull beneath the skin
> its sockets its machined teeth its seam.

Stepanova looks back across time and registers of language, from folk songs to canonical texts, and finds a seam, a crack, through which to peek into the past, through which to woo the dead:

> My features trickle through the bone like water.
> Put it in a sack.
> Put it in a pot.
> Grow basil from it.

 ILYA KAMINSKY

Often in these echoes one recognizes familiar patterns: "her history repeats and repeats itself". What is truly special (for me) here is that Stepanova is *actually* talking to the dead, seeking a tongue:

> Say the word that don't belong
> put it on and march along
> forget the old and step anew
> and the word will march with you

Some might consider Stepanova "a difficult poet". To my mind her "difficulty" lies not in some kind of extracurricular attempt at overt sophistication, but in the actual need to reflect the difficulty of her moment in time, its crisis, the culture's fragmentation. Her response to it is a fusion of various different cultures. Her response is a search for a new speech wherein the words convey to us more than their meanings signify. Which is to say, here is a spell in a time of our own particular cholera:

> A hand buried at Marne.
> A hand buried at Narva.
> A hand lying in the Galician wastes.
> The ash of a hand lying nowhere.
> All of this will return.

THE POET & TRANSLATOR

Maria Stepanova is a poet, essayist, journalist and the author of ten poetry collections and three books of essays. She has received several Russian and international literary awards, including the Andrey Bely Prize and Joseph Brodsky Fellowship. Her documentary novel *In Memory of Memory* (2017) won Russia's Big Book Award in 2018 and will be published by New Directions in the US and Fitzcarraldo in the UK. Stepanova is the founder and editor-in-chief of the online independent crowd-sourced journal *Colta.ru* which covers the cultural, social and political reality of contemporary Russia, reaching audiences of nearly a million visitors a month.

Sasha Dugdale has published five collections, including *Joy* (2017) and *Deformations* (2020). She won the 2016 Forward Prize for Best Single Poem. She specialises in translating contemporary Russian women poets and post-Soviet new writing for theatre. From 2012 to 2017 she was the editor of *Modern Poetry in Translation*. In 2020, she won an English PEN Translate Award. She is co-director of the biennial Winchester Poetry Festival and poet-in-residence at St John's College, Cambridge.

Image: Andrey Natotsinsky

EXTRACT FROM 'SPOLIA'

my brother said you're a fascist
you sing up, and I'll sing loud
we'll be back when the trees are in leaf
but I'll stand my ground

when the leaves are in fist
and the deer dances past the oak
the antifascist flips to fascist
and the wood goes for broke

words are attached to things
with old twine
and people lay down with their tubers
in the ground for all time

but them, they cross yards
with lists and chalk
and lick the paint off window sills
with tongues that fork

fascist fattish fetish
flatfish, flippery, facetious
but the air knows we're not of them,
none of you or us.

untie the words
let them lie desperate, without glory
and the wood will call back its men
non omnis moriar.

ISABELLE BAAFI

Isabelle Baafi is a writer and poet from London. She was the winner of the 2019 Vincent Cooper Literary Prize, and was shortlisted for the 2020 Bridport Prize and the 2019 Oxford Brookes International Poetry Competition. Her work has been published in *Poetry Review*, *Magma*, *Anthropocene, Finished Creatures, Tentacular* and *harana poetry*. She was a member of the 2019-20 London Library's Emerging Writers Programme, and the 2020 Griot's Well Programme with Writerz and Scribez. She is also an Obsidian Foundation Fellow and an Editor at *Magma*. Her debut pamphlet *Ripe* was published by ignitionpress.

IGNITION PRESS | £5.00 |

Ripe is a pamphlet which draws on the mundane to forge beauty, using sensual tones to deal with and address harsh subject matter. Baafi's poems are great inventions in terms of their use of form. Throughout this book, her use of language is never laboured in its endeavour to draw the reader's attention. The poems begin with an epigraph from Proverbs 27:7:

> to the hungry soul
> every bitter thing is sweet.

The full quote reads: "A sated man loathes honey, but to a famished man any bitter thing is sweet."

As such, this work expertly explores the hunger of existence from a physical, mental and emotional perspective. Baafi's poems render for us what seems like lived – or at least well-observed – experiences. Baafi uses the page like a roll of parchment and is confident to experiment with form, moving the reader's eyes both horizontally and vertically. This, when coupled with her use of vivid imagery, adds a significant depth and dimension to her poems. Poems such as 'hotboxing' are urgent, alluring and sing with electricity. The poet's gaze is searching for answers in the conscious world. That, too, is a form of hunger:

> Google Translate says your laugh means
> wandering echo

Overall, Baafi's poems often step outside the rational and waking consciousness in order to investigate other realms, be that paranoia, dream states etc. The unravelling of consciousness is referred to as a state of unbecoming:

> the patient is therefore most unbecoming
> the patient will soon unbecome completely

Through her lyric poems, prose poetry, erasures and much besides, Baafi offers us a complex world worth savouring, as she revels in language both sacred and profane. This is a pamphlet to enjoy and a poet to watch.

NICK MAKOHA & MARY JEAN CHAN

PLANTAIN

1.
Pick one with black skin. Plucked before it was
    ripe, left to darken on a windowsill, or garage crate,
        or in the pantry corner where secrets are born.

2.
Make sure it's plump. Squeeze it at the curves,
    weigh its resistance to your touch. Slice it with your
        tongue. Or, if this is your first time, the fingernail
            you use to pick your teeth. Keep the peel. Put it
                under your pillow and you will never be fruitless.

3.
Any oil will do, but make sure it knows the
    gluttony of heat. Pour just enough for each piece
        to tread the surface. Don't drown them.
            Give them hope. The hopeful taste the best.

4.
In the heat they will hiss, and some will spit.
    They will gather at the fringes, hide their bruising.
        Some will be too weak and fall apart. Others
            will stay hard around the edges. Do not
                be suspicious. This is how they endure the fire.

5.
Serve on a banana leaf, with the yam you pounded
    earlier, the ewe you slaughtered silently from behind.

HOLLY PESTER

Four years ago all I intended to do was write a long serious essay about sleeping bags. Or rather, about states of static stillness, latent with new life and plans, ridiculous in a way, rebellious in another, and the product of magical materials plus a work force. Poems about utopias, abortion and bogs seemed to come from this same impulse. The book's titular long poem of an abortion was written while staying in a house belonging to a nice woman who let artists occupy her old barn in the midlands of Ireland. Everyday I would walk through the surrounding bogland to feed a giant pig she had rescued and kept in a large shed about a mile from her house. I wrote about bogs while researching abortion rights protest songs in the Glasgow Women's Library. I camped alone on the Jurassic Coast and wrote about optimism. I stayed in an abandoned Soviet school building in Estonia and thought about butter. I went to the Communards' grave in Paris and wrote about sleeping bags, finally. I went to work a lot, I moved house four times. I tried very hard to think about Hegel's theory of history and watched a lot of Marilyn Monroe films. My age turned into something else. I loved Spinoza's notion of the survival of thought and Blake's ideas about preservation. This book sees a lot of ideas held by materials that then become an idea, held by another material. We (Rachael and I) structured the book in 'acts' as a nod to the genres of times a life lives through, in eccentric and dramatically timed narratives, only sometimes funny but always comic.

Holly Pester is a poet and writer. She has worked in sound art and performance, with BBC Radio, Women's Art Library and The Wellcome Collection. Holly has published pamphlets and mixed media works including *Go to reception and ask for Sara in red felt tip* (Book Works, 2015) and *Common Rest* (Prototype, 2016). Her poem 'Comic Timing' was shortlisted for the Forward Prize for Best Single Poem in 2019.

HOLLY RECOMMENDS

Work and Days, Bernadette Mayer (New Directions); *Yes I am a Destroyer*, Mira Matter (Ma Bibliothèque); *Guitar!*, Sarah Tripp (Book works); *Scammer*, Dom Hale (the87 Press); *simmering of a declarative void*, Robert Kiely (the87 Press); *Romance of the End*, Elaine Kahn (Soft Skull); *Notes on the Sonnets*, Luke Kennard (Penned in the Margins); *Special Subcommittee*, Samuel Soloman (Commune Editions); *Click Away Close Door Say*, Verity Spott (Contraband); *States of the Body Produced by Love*, Nisha Ramayya (Ignota); *Other Life*, Ed Luker (Broken Sleep); *Socialist Realism*, Trisha Low (Emily Books) and *of sirens, body & faultlines*, Nat Raha (Boiler House).

COMIC TIMING

GRANTA | £10.99 | PBS PRICE £8.25

Holly Pester's debut collection *Comic Timing* offers an astounding range of peculiar, smart and inventive poems. Poems which accommodate multiple curiosities. Arguments built around anecdotes, musings, events and impossibilities, all working in tandem to distort and subvert the safety of conventionality. The title poem reads as a somewhat deadpan yet heartfelt voyage centred around an early medical abortion. At other points the writing borrows from the essay, the monologue and song. 'The Work and its Record' presents as an overwhelming and garrulous block of text, an assortment of modes, woven artfully together by incessant conjunctions which allude to gender roles.

> You can't separate the work of cutting and gluing the newspaper clippings and organising the meetings and chairing and note taking and making the tea and cataloguing and nursing and protesting and caring and nurturing...

Emphasis on the politics of gender, reproductive rights, bodily autonomy and desire become recurring motifs in much of Pester's work. One striking feature throughout is her ability to layer poems with highly original and intriguing imagery. This particular moment from the poem 'Aborted' stayed with me for some time:

> Ask me. Do I end here. I fail. I drink a foot. I ask the wall

The abrupt tone parted by full stops invokes a kind of bifurcation concerning the human body and its ability to sustain life, or the parts we feel more comfortable to celebrate. The antipode being fetishisation, shame and eating disorders, all of which seem to be alluded to.

Pester's ability to move through poems with verve and latitude means the writing is never static, even while being mordant or irreverent, it manages to appear justified and earnt. A cross-pollination of theory, experimentation, form and realism, *Comic Timing* is an illuminating read.

 ANTHONY ANAXAGOROU

COMMON GRAVES, THE BODY AND THE BLOCKADE

A writer doesn't know where her husband's grave is
has an affair with a gravedigger.

She dreams of him and starts to treat her dreams as places
to understand what prison is.
She meets him at night by drowning in her sleep.

She calls the ritual 'plunging under'

she found his blood in the finished story:
coward   traitor   fascist   a forest

and now my loneliness is a book of him

but The Writers
The writers are on fire

in residence
and preserved

SPRING BOOK REVIEWS

Inhale/Exile is a striking debut poetry collection by Abeer Ameer, a rising poet of Iraqi heritage, who lives in Cardiff. Inspired by the many stories she heard as a child and visiting family in Iraq as an adult, *Inhale/Exile* offers us lyrical histories, stories of courage, dedication and love. It is also an examination of collective grief and a reflection of unrest, on a scale that is both cinematic and intimate. These are poems of "Aluminium pots almost large enough to hold her sorrow", and "words only heard by ants and God".

FEBRUARY | SEREN | £9.99 | PBS PRICE £7.50

FLEUR ADCOCK: THE MERMAID'S PURSE

This eclectic ensemble from celebrated poet Fleur Adcock dances through the landscapes and histories of New Zealand and Britain. Adcock's adroit, witty verse is a joy to read, and *Mermaid's Purse* is completed by a moving sequence in memory of Roy Fisher, honouring her friend with a turn of phrase everyone would wish to be memorialized by: "gifted with wits, with wit, with a brain / that these witless times can't easily spare".

FEBRUARY | BLOODAXE | £10.99 | PBS PRICE £8.25

KHAIRANI BAROKKA: ULTIMATUM ORANGUTAN

In this searing second collection Khairani Barokka examines her Indonesian heritage and the aftermath of colonialism, "thinly-muffled / genocide", in an attempt "to undo each spool of violence". Intersecting trauma and injustice, these poems also tackle climate change and extinction with an infectious rage. But beneath these global concerns lies the body politic; a probing exposé of "abled assumptions" and discrimination: "I sit in the wonky wheelchair museum's provided".

MARCH | NINE ARCHES PRESS | £9.99 | PBS PRICE £7.50

This is a rollicking romp through the downright daft, playful and existential from Twitter's unofficial Poet Laureate. Bilston throws the poetry rule book out the window: "Poetry does not have to rhyme. / Well, at least not ~~all the time~~ always." Revelling in spoonerisms and idioms, this is a tour-de-force of Spike Milligan-esque silliness that's guaranteed to convert even the most reluctant of readers to poetry!

JANUARY | PICADOR | £12.99 | PBS PRICE £9.75

SUPRIYA KAUR DHALIWAL: THE YAK DILEMMA

The Yak Dilemma by Supriya Kaur Dhaliwal takes a sharp look at what it means to belong somewhere. Dhaliwal's subjects are family, displacement, language and the ironies of modern life. Her work is quick, interrogative and moves deceptively easily from city to city and subject to subject, but never do we lose sight of the questions Dhaliwal asks, "Where have I truly come to?"

FEBRUARY | MAKINA BOOKS | £10.00 | PBS PRICE £7.50

CAROL ANN DUFFY: EMPTY NEST

In this moving anthology of 99 poems, former Poet Laureate Carol Ann Duffy explores the timeless bond of parent and child: "Dear child, the house pines when you leave." Both tender and humorous, this selection combines classic poets with modern greats from Simon Armitage to Shakespeare. Perfect for all those parents encountering an empty nest for the first time, this is a celebration of new freedoms and a lesson in the art of losing. As Penelope Shuttle writes, "Just as I work out how to be a mother / she stops being a child."

FEBRUARY | PICADOR | £14.99 (HB) | PBS PRICE £11.25

SPRING BOOK REVIEWS

Divided into two parts After and Before the great unspoken shift of the current lockdown era, *The Oscillations* provides a fitting companion to the strange times we live in. It is notable that there is no false nostalgia for bygone days here; Fox does not shy away from the troubles of past years and how they guided us to this point, but there is also hopefulness and a beauty of language which lifts the reader from the surrounding darkness.

FEBRUARY | NINE ARCHES PRESS | £9.99 | PBS PRICE £7.50

KIRSTEN LUCKINS: PASSERINE

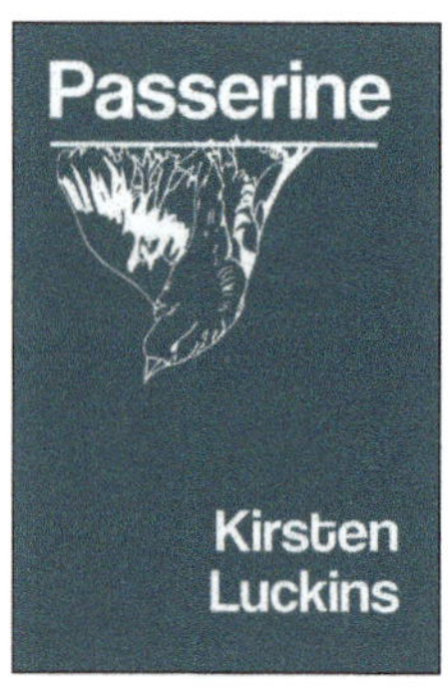

Passerine is an elegiac collection, as concerned with the fierce beauty of the natural world as it is with grief, healing and friendship. *Passerine* is written as a series of letters to a single subject and we move through the seasons with poems that are by turns funny, "Dear Sophie, / if I ever use the word petrichor / just shoot me", and heartbreaking –"he is growing up so blonde without you."

FEBRUARY | BAD BETTY PRESS | £10.00 | PBS PRICE £7.50

BEN OKRI: A FIRE IN MY HEAD

A Fire in My Head burns with a dazzling array of visionary poems on social justice by the renowned Booker Prize winning author and Nigerian born poet Ben Okri. These electrifying and highly topical poems tackle everything from racism to Grenfell Tower and Covid-19. This is a timely reminder that "ignorance will destroy this world with hate / wisdom with light will change that fate".

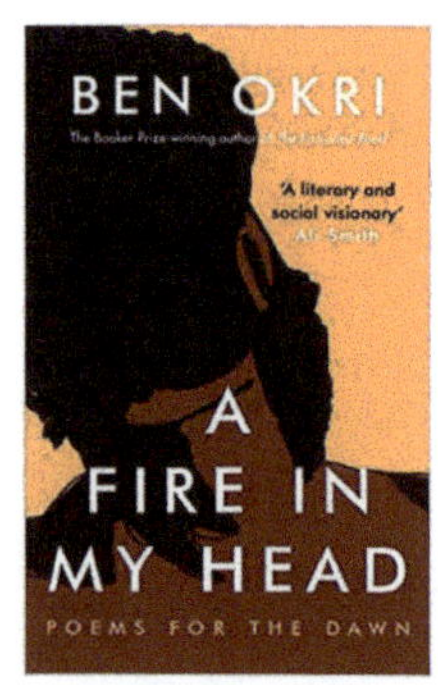

JANUARY | HEAD OF ZEUS | £9.99 | PBS PRICE £7.50

Poems by the suffragette and activist Sylvia Pankhurst are republished here by Smokestack books after almost a century. As Chris Searle says, in his introduction, these are poems that have been produced from "sheer, unrelenting and permanent activism". Pankhurst's poetry rings with urgency and documents her life and work, including her time in Holloway Prison. Now, as when they were written, they call for a fairer, less punitive world.

FEBRUARY | SMOKESTACK | £7.99 | PBS PRICE £6.00

Willson's second collection is effortlessly transportive. These poems swirl through a bygone age of shipping, of Essex and its coasts and marshes, to the life of a woman lost to time named Eliza, recorded only in a piece of old news-print. *Fleet* suddenly leaps forward a hundred years to consider the process of change and the windows on the past which historical records grant us. This is rich, heady verse, evocatively catapulting the reader through time and space.

FEBRUARY | CARCANET | £11.99 | PBS PRICE £9.00

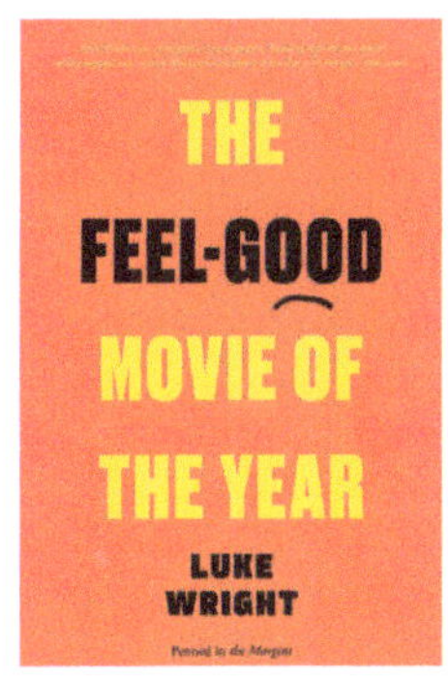

The spoken word poet and performer Luke Wright turns his attention to divorce, parenthood and politics as "a single parent on the Brexit coast". In these raw and honest poems, Wright "wear(s) (his) sadness" on his sleeve with aching candour. At turns hilarious and deeply moving, *The Feel-Good Movie of the Year* tackles anxiety, "that blowsy bully", and the slow process of healing – gradually lowering the "drawbridge" to let people in.

MARCH | PENNED IN THE MARGINS | £9.99 | PBS PRICE £7.50

SPRING PAMPHLETS

Aubade After a French Movie by Zoë Brigley is a love letter to female sexuality, guided by the spirit of the Medieval Welsh poet, Gwerful Mechain. Brigley's translations of Mechain are sexy, irreverent and playful: "what I see is enough / for you to be my bae". These poems are deeply relevant for today, questioning why it is still discouraged for women to openly discuss their bodies and desires.

BROKEN SLEEP BOOKS | £6.00 |

ELLA DUFFY: ROOTSTALK

Hazel Press is an exciting new independent publisher with a focus on the environment and climate change. Ella Duffy's intriguing pamphlet takes the form of twisting accounts and dialogues shared by historical and mythological female figures, including Persephone, Esther and Demeter. These voices shift and intertwine around botanical images, ghost orchids, mushrooms, ferns and cow parsley. At once ethereal and startlingly sharp of phrase, this is a beautiful pamphlet to become lost within.

HAZEL PRESS | £10.00 |

CARRIE ETTER: THE SHOOTING GALLERY

A sequence of prose-poems inspired by the Czech surrealist and transgender artist Toyen's lithograph series, *The Shooting Gallery.* Carrie Etter uses these works of art as a lens to examine the gun-violence routinely committed in US schools and universities. Each of the poems in the second part is dedicated to the site of such shootings. Mournful and disturbing, this is a profound and powerful pamphlet from the ever innovative Verve Press.

VERVE PRESS | £7.50 |

ROZ GODDARD: LOST CITY

The former Birmingham Poet Laureate Roz Goddard presents a sequence of poems set in an imagined post-industrial city. Tour Guides and quirky characters lead us through this lost city, "looking / for sudden things". At once mythic and familiar, these vignettes examine the aftermath of toxic leadership, political collapse and not-so-distant dystopia: "Trapped for so long / in the small room of leaning guitars / I forgot the sky". All of this is hauntingly illustrated by Emma Dai'an Wright.

THE EMMA PRESS | £5.00 |

IAN McMILLAN: YES BUT WHAT IS THIS? WHAT EXACTLY?

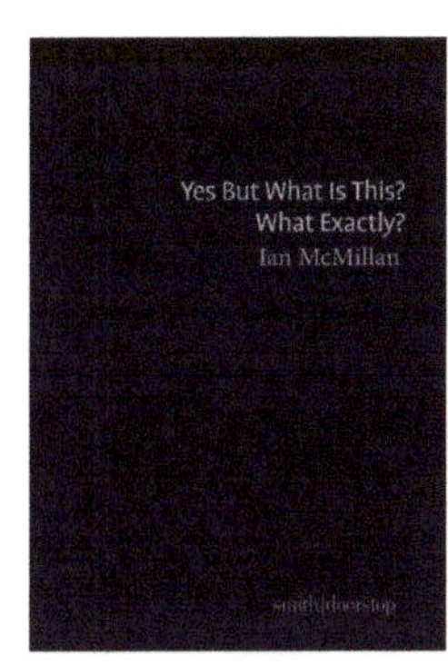

National Treasure and presenter of BBC Radio 3's *The Verb*, Ian McMillan, brings his irrepressible wit and energy to this pre-pandemic pamphlet. Written long before Covid-19, these are uplifting and insightful poems, but beneath the levity lies a deeply political interrogation of the financial crisis and homelessness. This is no rose-tinted elegy to the Old Normal but a reminder of life as it always was, both complex and joyous.

SMITH | DOORSTOP | £6.00 |

RICKY RAY: THE SOUND OF THE EARTH SINGING TO HERSELF

The Sound of the Earth Singing to Herself by Ricky Ray is a pamphlet that stands in awe of the beauty of the natural world. Contained within it are portraits of rural America, disability and loss; dog walks, sparrows and the earth as something intensely alive. It is summed up best in his poem '(Dis)ability' where Ray writes, "Some days, my body is so beautiful / I can't believe I get to live here."

FLY ON THE WALL | £7.99 |

SPRING BOOK LISTINGS

AUTHOR	TITLE	PUBLISHER	RRP
Fleur Adcock	The Mermaid's Purse	Bloodaxe Books	£10.99
Abeer Ameer	Inhale/Exile	Seren	£9.99
Tiffany Atkinson	Lumen	Bloodaxe Books	£10.99
Khairani Barokka	Ultimatum, Orangutan	Nine Arches Press	£9.99
Victoria Barragan	Mirror Lake, Waxen Swan	Knives Forks Spoons	£8.00
Brian Bilston	Alexa, what is there to know about love?	Picador	£12.99
Charles Boyle	The Disguise: Selected Poems	Carcanet Press	£12.99
Jo Brandon	Cures	Valley Press	£9.99
Moya Cannon	Selected Poems	Carcanet Press	£16.99
Amit Chaudhuri	Ramanujan	Shearsman Books	£10.95
Lucy Harvest Clarke	A Light Worker	Broken Sleep Books	£8.99
Ned Denny	B (After Dante)	Carcanet Press	£16.99
Supriya Kaur Dhaliwal	The Yak Dilemma	Makina Books	£10.00
Carol Duffy Ann (Editor)	The Empty Nest	Picador	£14.99
Claire Dyer	Yield	Two Rivers Press	£9.99
Kate Fox	The Oscillations	Nine Arches Press	£9.99
Annie Freud	Hiddensee	Picador	£10.99
Angela Gardner	The Sorry Tale of the Mignonette	Shearsman Books	£12.95
Salena Godden	Mrs Death Misses Death	Canongate	£14.99
Derek Gromadzki	Horology	Shearsman Books	£10.95
Jen Hadfield	The Stone Age	Picador	£10.95
Rosalind Hudis	Restorations	Seren	£9.99
Cyril Jones, Philip Gross	Troeon/Turnings	Seren	£12.99
Victoria Kennefick	Eat or We Both Starve	Carcanet Press	£10.99
Aaron Kent (Editor)	Crossing Lines: Anthology of immigrant poetry	Broken Sleep Books	£7.99
August Kleinzahler	Snow Approaching on the Hudson	Faber & Faber	£10.99
Angela Leighton	One, Two	Carcanet Press	£12.99
Kirsten Luckins	Passerine	Bad Betty Press	£10.00
Aoife Lyall	Mother, Nature	Bloodaxe Books	£9.95
John McAuliffe & Michael Schmidt (Editors)	New Poetries VIII: An Anthology	Carcanet Press	£14.99
Gill McEvoy	Are You Listening?	Hedgehog Poetry Press	£10.99
Ben Okri	A Fire in My Head	Head of Zeus	£9.99
Sylvia Pankhurst	Writ on Cold Slate	Smokestack	£7.99
Holly Pester	Comic Timing	Granta	£10.99
Rowan Ricardo Phillips	Living Weapon	Faber & Faber	£10.99
Jenna Plewes	A Woven Rope	V. Press	£10.99
Wendy Pratt	When I Think of My Body as a Horse	The Poetry Buisiness	£9.95
Yousif M. Qasmiyeh	Writing the Camp	Broken Sleep Books	£10. 99
Michael Roberts Symmons	Ransom	Cape	£10.00
Michael Schmidt	Talking to Stanley on the Telephone	The Poetry Buisiness	£9.95
John Sewell	Woods River Road	Fair Acre Press	£9.99
Nathan Shepherdson	how to spear sleep	Shearsman Books	£10.95
Ruth Stacey	Viola the Virgin Queen	Knives Forks Spoons	£10.00
Lesley Storm	It's About Time	Leamington Books	£9.99
G.C. Waldrep	The Earliest Witnesses	Carcanet Press	£12.99
Simon Williams	The Magpie Almanac	Dempsey & Windle	£10.00
Isobel Williams	Shibari Carmina: Catullus	Carcanet Press	£14.99
Judith Willson	Fleet	Carcanet Press	£11.99
Luke Wright	The Feel-Good Movie of the Year	Penned in the Margins	£9.99
George Ttoouli	from Animal Illicit	Broken Sleep Books	£8.99
Various	Myth & Metamorphosis	Penteract Press	£10.00
Michael Vince	The Long Distance	Mica Press	£8.99
Andrea Witzke Slot	The Ministry of Flowers	Valley Press	£12.00

TRANSLATIONS

AUTHOR	TITLE	PUBLISHER	RRP
Chawki Abdelamir, trans. Alan Dent	Attempts on Death	Smokestack Books	£8.99
René Noyau, trans. Gerard Noyau with Peter Pegnall	Earth on Fire	Two Rivers Press	£12.00
Seán Ó Ríordáin, trans. Greg Delanty	Apathy Is Out	Bloodaxe Books	£12.99
Maria Stepanova, trans. Sasha Dugdale	War of the Beasts and the Animals	Bloodaxe Books	£12.00
Pia Tafdrup, trans. David McDuff	The Taste of Steel, The Smell of Snow	Bloodaxe Books	£12.99

PAMPHLETS

AUTHOR	TITLE	PUBLISHER	RRP
Isabelle Baafi	Ripe	ignitonpress	£5.00
Miranda Barnes Lynn	Blue Dot Aubade	V. Press	£6.50
Claire Booker	The Bone That Sang	Indigo Dreams	£6.00
Penny Boxhall & woodcuts by Naoko Matsubara	In Praise of Hands	Ashmolean Museum	£9.95
Zoë Brigley	Aubade After a French Movie	Broken Sleep Books	£6.50
Matthew Caley	Prophecy is Easy	Blueprint Press	£6.00
S.D. Curtis	Diary of a Divorce	Arc Publications	£7.00
Lucia Damacela Orellana	InHERent	Fly on the Wall	£7.99
Ella Duffy	Rootstalk	Hazel Press	£10.00
Carrie Etter	The Shooting Gallery	Verve Poetry Press	£7.50
Daniel Fraser	Lung Iron	ignitonpress	£5.00
Roz Goddard	Lost City	Emma Press	£5.00
Matthew Hollis	Leaves	Hazel Press	£10.00
Ian McMillan	Yes But What Is This? What Exactly?	The Poetry Business	£6.00
Middex	Perpetual Skip	Makina Books	£8.00
Steph Morris	Please don't trample us; we are trying to grow!	Fair Acre Press	£7.50
J.L.M. Morton	Lake 32	Yew Tree Press	£5.00
Nicholas Murray	A Quartet in Winter	Rack Press	£5.00
Miriam Nash	The Nine Mothers of Heimdallr	Hercules Editions	£10.00
Shazea Quraishi	The Taxidermist	Verve Poetry Press	£7.50
Ricky Ray	The Sound of the Earth Singing To Herself	Fly on the Wall Press	£7.99
Kathrin Schmidt	Twenty Poems	Arc Publications	£6.00
Anna Selby	Field Notes	Hazel Press	£10.00
Kathryn Southworth	No Man's Land	Dempsey & Windle	£8.00
Laura Theis	how to extricate yourself	Dempsey & Windle	£8.00
Kostya Tsolakis	Ephebos	ignitonpress	£5.00
U.G. Világos	Collected Experimentalisms 1993-1996	Broken Sleep Books	£6.50
Sue Wallace-Shaddad	A City Waking Up	Dempsey & Windle	£8.00
Sarah Wallis	Medusa Retold	Fly on the Wall Press	£5.99
Lynn Woollacott	Judy, Out of the Box	Dempsey & Windle	£8.00
Cliff Yates	Birmingham Canal Navigation	Knives Forks Spoons	£6.50

www.ingramcontent.com/pod-product-compliance
Lightning Source LLC
LaVergne TN
LVHW052238150726
843469LV00055B/2237